ARMORED DINOSAURS

PATRICK SCAFIDI

APPLESAUCE
PRESS

Kennebunkport, ME

13-Digit ISBN: 978-1604336009
10-Digit ISBN: 1604336005

This book may be ordered by mail from the publisher. Please include $5.99 for postage and handling.
Please support your local bookseller first!

Books published by Cider Mill Press Book Publishers are available at special discounts for bulk purchases in the United States by corporations, institutions, and other organizations. For more information, please contact the publisher.

Applesauce Press is an imprint of
Cider Mill Press Book Publishers
"Where good books are ready for press"
PO Box 454
12 Spring Street
Kennebunkport, Maine 04046

Visit us on the Web!
www.cidermillpress.com

Cover and interior design by Tango Media
Typography: Destroy, Gipsiero, PMN Caecilia, Block Berthold

Image Credits: see page 58

Printed in China

1 2 3 4 5 6 7 8 9 0
First Edition

CONTENTS

WHAT IS AN ARMORED DINOSAUR? 8

WHY DID DINOSAURS HAVE ARMOR? 10

WERE THERE DIFFERENT KINDS OF ARMOR? 12

HOW BIG WERE ARMORED DINOSAURS? 14

WHAT DID ARMORED DINOSAURS EAT? 17

DID ARMORED DINOSAURS HAVE ANY PREDATORS? 18

THE STEGOSAURIA FAMILY 21

THE ANKYLOSAURIA FAMILY 33

OTHER ARMORED DINOSAURS 44

TRUE OR FALSE QUIZ 54

GLOSSARY 56

WHAT IS AN ARMORED DINOSAUR?

Life on Earth has always come down to one basic struggle: that between a predator and its prey. During the Age of Dinosaurs, that struggle was at its most extreme. With predators like T. rex roaming the land, most dinosaurs could only hope to hide or flee. But some dinosaurs evolved so impressively that they were often able to fight off their hungry predators—or at least discourage them from attacking. We refer to these creatures as "armored dinosaurs."

While almost every dinosaur possessed armor of some sort, the armored dinosaurs we refer to today belonged to *Thyreophora*. The most famous members of *Thyreophora* were the *Ankylosaurus* and *Stegosaurus*, but almost all of the hundreds of tank-like dinosaurs got their armor from closely fused *osteoderms*— bony deposits underneath the skin that formed hard scales, spikes, plates—even helmets! And that came in handy, because these short-limbed *quadrupeds*, or four-legged creatures, would have had a tough time outrunning any predator.

An Ankylosaurus
drinks from a pool.

WHY DID DINOSAURS HAVE ARMOR?

We know that dinosaurs developed armor as a way to defend themselves from predators, but the armor found on *Thyreophora* was truly special. Their defense systems allowed these dinosaurs to live a long time—longer than some predators, if they lived carefully.

Of course, armor had other uses as well. Occasionally, the sight of their armor would be enough to keep predators away. Other times, armored dinosaurs would fight one another for territory, locking their horns and spikes in fierce battles. Larger spikes or more impressive armor would also make a dinosaur more attractive to potential mates.

A Postosuchus *tries to attack* a *heavily-armored* Desmatosuchus.

WERE THERE DIFFERENT KINDS OF ARMOR?

Not every had dinosaur a full set of armor, but every armored dinosaur had similar characteristics. *Osteoderms* made their skin tough against sharp teeth, and most tails had some weapon near the tip. For some, this meant a heavy club they would swing with alarming speed; for others, sharp spikes that cleared the space around the dinosaur.

The defense systems didn't stop there. Many dinosaurs contained extra plates around their skulls and chest, giving them a helmet or 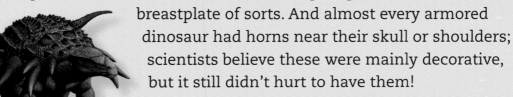 breastplate of sorts. And almost every armored dinosaur had horns near their skull or shoulders; scientists believe these were mainly decorative, but it still didn't hurt to have them!

HOW BIG WERE ARMORED DINOSAURS?

5 FEET, 9 INCHES

6 FEET TALL

Ankylosaur

25 FEET LONG

Armored dinosaurs varied in size depending on their place in the evolutionary timeline and their surrounding environment.

Stegosaurs could grow up to 10 feet tall and 30 feet long, weighing almost 3.5 tons!

Ankylosaurs could grow up to 6 feet tall and 25 feet long, weighing nearly 6.5 tons!

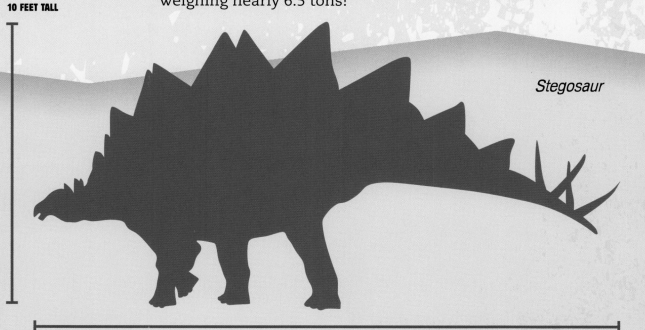

10 FEET TALL

Stegosaur

30 FEET LONG

A herd of Sauropelta *dinosaurs graze in a woodland.*

WHAT DID ARMORED DINOSAURS EAT?

Almost all armored dinosaurs were herbivores, but scientists think they might have eaten insects too, due to their similarities to armadillos and hedgehogs. Still, the lack of strong forelimbs and sharp teeth suggest that most armored dinosaurs stayed truly vegetarian.

As most *Thyreophora*—but especially *ankylosaurs*—had short forelimbs, we assume that they fed exclusively on low-growing vegetation that required less competition with other dinosaurs.

DID ARMORED DINOSAURS HAVE ANY PREDATORS?

What's the point of all that armor if you aren't defending against anything? Yes, the life of an armored dinosaur was no picnic. While the armor itself could stop some predators, it was often tested. Fossils often show signs of intense battles, including broken or missing spikes buried into the fossil of a predator. Whether being attacked from the air or on the ground, these roaming tanks needed constant protection.

A Stegosaurus *defends itself from two* Torvosaurus.

A Stegosaurus roams its habitat.

STEGOSAURIA

Stegosaurs are probably the most famous armored dinosaurs. They are part of the *Stegosauria* group and lived almost entirely during the Jurassic Era.

These herbivores are best known for the plates or spines running down their backs—a surefire way to keep flying predators from aerial attacks. But a *stegosaur*'s strongest asset was not its spiny back, but its tail. Spiky, long, and surprisingly agile, a *stegosaur*'s tail was its fiercest weapon against potential predators—even the occasional *Allosaurus*, their fiercest pursuer. This grouping of spikes is called the *thagomizer*.

So why vertical back plates? Scientists have a few ideas. These plates made all *stegosaurs* look more intimidating by increasing their size, which kept enemies from bothering with them. They also frightened predators, attracted mates, and maybe even helped the dinosaurs absorb heat from the sun.

STEGOSAURUS STENOPS

STEG-oh-SAWR-us

REGION: Northern USA

SIZE: 30 feet

AGE: 150-155 million years

DIET: Herbivore

SCIENCE BITE: With large, upright plates stretching down its back, *Stegosaurus stenops* is perhaps the most recognizable armored dinosaur of all time. Its name means "roofed lizard," referring to its shingle-like plates. Originally believed to be a form of armor, these plates likely just served as deterrents to predators—increasing its apparent height and attracting it to potential mates. In addition to these plates, *Stegosaurus* also had an impressive tail with four sharp spikes and *osteoderms* on its neck to protect its throat. Despite its massive size, *Stegosaurus* possessed a tiny brain—about the size of a dog's.

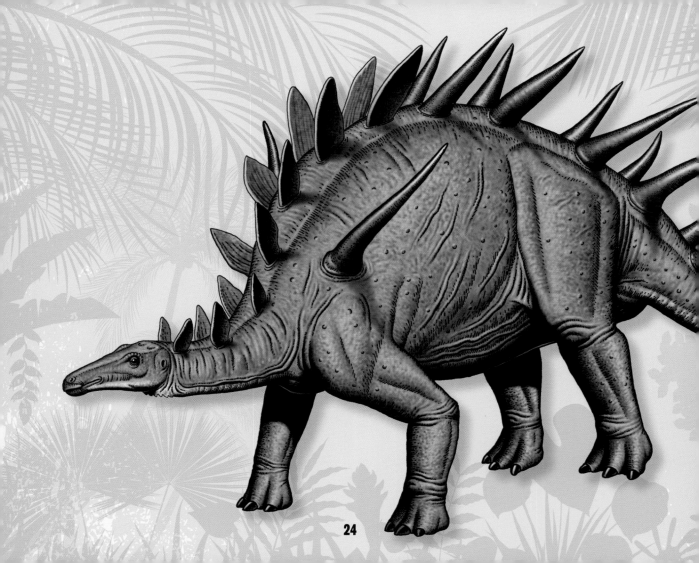

KENTROSAURUS AETHIOPICUS

KENT-row-SAWR-us

REGION: Tanzania

SIZE: 16 feet

AGE: 150–155 million years

DIET: Herbivore

SCIENCE BITE: *Kentrosaurus aethiopicus* had both plates and spikes running down its back, which sets it apart from most other *stegosaurs*. While not quite as large as its other family members, *Kentrosaurus* would have been nearly impossible to attack from behind. Its especially spiky tail had at least 40 vertebrae, making it incredibly flexible and especially dangerous to predators.

WUERHOSAURUS HOMHENI

WHERE-ho-SAWR-us

REGION: China, Mongolia

SIZE: 23 feet

AGE: 100 million years

DIET: Herbivore

SCIENCE BITE: Though scientists have only recovered partial skeletons, *Wuerhosaurus homheni* is particularly interesting because, unlike its Jurassic family members, this dinosaur lived in the early Cretaceous—making it the last known surviving stegosaur!

Despite the partial fossil recovery, it is widely accepted that *Wuerhosaurus* had armor similar to the *Stegosaurus*—large plates on its back and sharp spikes on its tail. This dinosaur appears to have been even lower to the ground than its ancestors, suggesting it adapted to access the lowest possible vegetation.

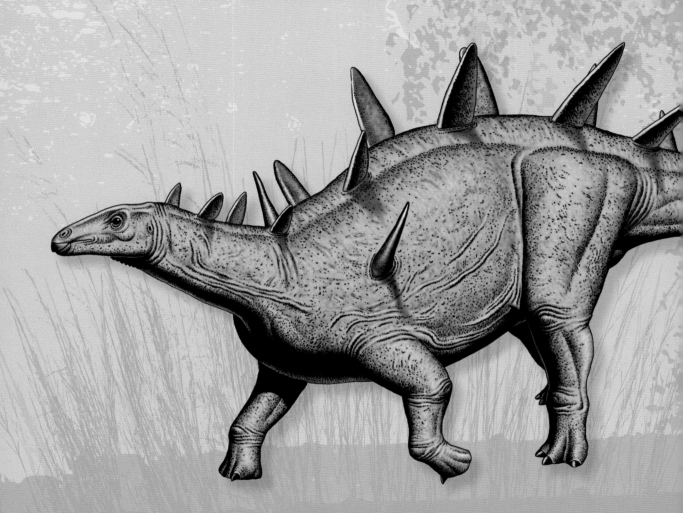

TUOJIANGOSAURUS MULTISPINUS

TOE-hwang-oh-SAWR-us

REGION: China

SIZE: 25 feet long

AGE: 160 million years

DIET: Herbivore

SCIENCE BITE: This was the first *stegosaur* to be discovered in China, and despite its old age, it's one of the *stegosaurs* we know the most about due to its nearly complete skeletal remains.

Named "Tuo River Lizard" for its original site of discovery, *Tuojiangosaurus multispinus* had spikes on both its tail and its shoulders—making it difficult to attack from any angle. These dinosaurs also had very distinct triangular plates on its back.

HUAYANGOSAURUS TAIBAII

HWA-yang-oh-SAWR-us

REGION: China

SIZE: Up to 15 feet long

AGE: 165 million years

DIET: Herbivore

SCIENCE BITE: *Huayangosaurus taibaii* is the earliest known *stegosaur* ever discovered, with fossils dating back at least 20 million years before the first *Stegosaurus*. In addition to being very old, *Huayangosaurus* was very small—no more than 15 feet long.

With rows of spiky plates on its back and a thagomizer of two sets of spikes, *Huayangosaurus* could still be a threatening opponent despite its size. But its relatively tiny plates probably didn't help too much against determined hunters and likely offered little additional sun absorption—leading scientists to believe they were purely decorative.

The old stegosaur *fossils found in China* led to a *theory among scientists that* Stegosaurs *originated in China before traveling across the land bridge to North America during the Jurassic Period.*

A Saichania chulsanensis *roams its habitat.*

ANKYLOSAURIA

Though perhaps not as well known as the *Stegosauria*, members of *Ankylosauria* had the best defenses evolution could offer.

Big, heavy, and slow—these dinosaurs didn't bother fleeing their predators. And with their complex armor systems, that's no surprise.

Nearly covered in armor from head to toe, most *ankylosaurids* had tough, bony *osteoderms* along their backs, two (or more) front-facing horns, and extra plates of bone covering anywhere from the skull to the chest to even the eyelids!

An *ankylosaur's* greatest weapon, though, was its tail. Like the *stegosaurs* before it, ankylosaurids had vicious tails they would use in any threatening situation. But unlike the *stegosaurs*, these were not spiky tails—they were clubs, reinforced with several layers of bone and swung with thundering power. Scientists believe the bigger tails could break the bones of a *T. rex*, when swung with enough force.

With walnut-sized brains mirroring those of its *stegosaur* cousins, these dinosaurs were not smart, and they didn't have to be. With their defense system, they could enjoy their diet of vegetation in relative peace.

ANKYLOSAURUS MAGNIVENTRIS

ANN-kie-lo-SAWR-us

REGION: USA, Canada

SIZE: Up to 25 feet long

AGE: 66 to 68 million years

DIET: Herbivore

SCIENCE BITE: The most familiar member of its group, and the dinosaur after which the entire subgroup is named, *Ankylosaurus magniventris* is the most well defended dinosaur ever discovered. But despite all this, we haven't found many fossils. In fact, scientists have never recovered a complete skeleton. Still, its relatively recent existence—*Ankylosaurus* was one of the last dinosaurs living before the extinction event— has allowed researchers to learn a lot about this armored dinosaur.

If *Ankylosaurus* wasn't the largest of its family, it was close. And its bulk was only a small part of its defense. Even this dinosaur's

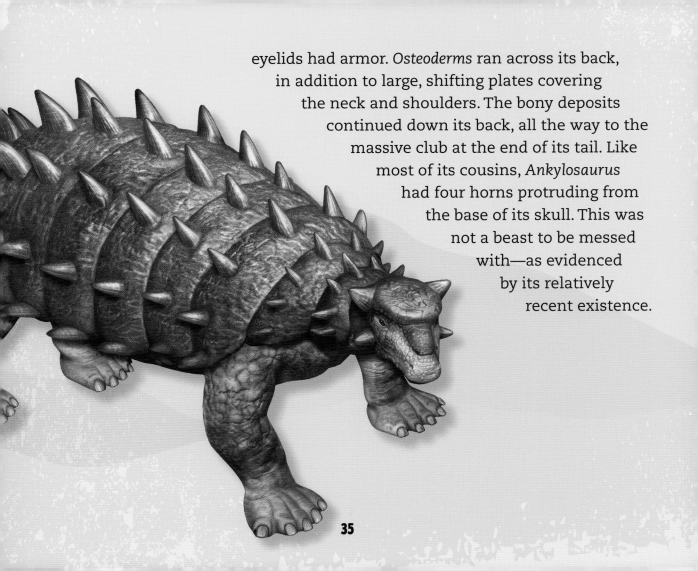

eyelids had armor. *Osteoderms* ran across its back,
in addition to large, shifting plates covering
the neck and shoulders. The bony deposits
continued down its back, all the way to the
massive club at the end of its tail. Like
most of its cousins, *Ankylosaurus*
had four horns protruding from
the base of its skull. This was
not a beast to be messed
with—as evidenced
by its relatively
recent existence.

EUOPLOCEPHALUS TUTUS

YOU-oh-ploe-SEFF-ah-luss

REGION: Canada and northern USA

SIZE: 20 feet long

AGE: 75 - 77 million years

DIET: Herbivore

SCIENCE BITE: With a name that means "well-armored head," it's no surprise that *Euoplocephalus tutus* was particularly tough from the neck up. Bony eyelids, two bony rings around its neck, and a short (but sharp) beak show how this dinosaur earned its name. Beyond its skull, this huge *ankylosaur* had short spikes formed by *osteoderms* along its back and its family's clubbed tail.

Scientists have long debated how many *Euoplocephalus* fossils have been found. While initially considered one of the most common *ankylosaurid* fossils, the number of authenticated *Euoplocephalus* remains has since been lowered to about 15.

GASTONIA BURGEI

gas-TONE-ee-ah

REGION: USA (Utah)

SIZE: About 17 feet long

AGE: 125 million years

DIET: Herbivore

SCIENCE BITE: Though *Gastonia burgei* is often labeled a *nodosaur*, scientists have disagreed on this point. With large spikes on its back and tail—a decidedly non-*nodosaurian* trait—this dinosaur would have been incredibly difficult to attack from above.

    Gasontia's main threat was the *Utahraptor*, a predator at the same time and location. Plenty of *Gastonia* remains have been discovered, suggesting that the raptors preferred to focus on other, less well-defended prey.

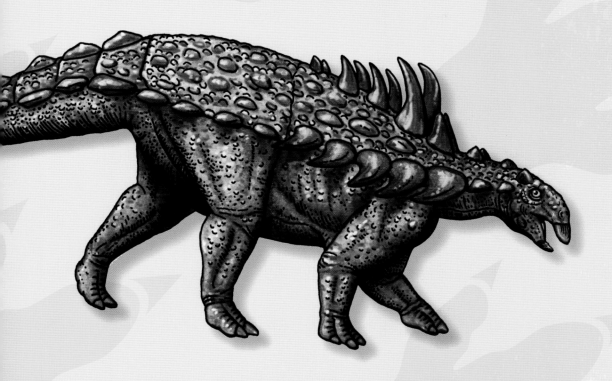

A Panoplosaurus *wanders by two* Ornithomimus.

40

PANOPLOSAURUS MIRUS

PAN-oh-ploh-SAWR-us

REGION: Canada

SIZE: 23 feet long and nearly 4 tons

AGE: 76 million years

DIET: Herbivore

SCIENCE BITE: A proper *nodosaur*, *Panoplosaurus mirus* was still an incredibly well-defended lizard despite its lack of a clubbed tail. And that should come as no surprise, as its name translates to "completely armored lizard." It had *osteoderms* covering its neck, back and tail; long armor plates on its neck, shoulders and forelimbs; head armor fused like a helmet—even reinforced cheek bones! This dinosaur was so well protected that it's believed it charged defensively like a rhinoceros.

41

EDMONTONIA LONGICEPS

ED-mon-TONE-ee-ah

REGION: Canada

SIZE: 22 feet long

AGE: 69 - 76 million years

DIET: Herbivore

SCIENCE BITE: Not only did *Edmontonia longiceps* have *osteoderms* down its back, but also large spikes protruding from the side of its body. The four largest spikes came just above the shoulder. Despite their threatening appearance, the large spikes were likely used in territorial fights. This dinosaur was named after the Edmonton Formation in Canada, where it was found.

OTHER ARMORED DINOSAURS

While *Stegosauria* and *Ankylosauria* are the two most advanced subgroups in *Thyreophora*, they were hardly the only ones. Plenty of other dinosaurs fall into the "armored" category, though their specific place in the group has been the subject of debate for over a hundred years. This is made more complicated by the fact that some of these "black sheep" existed long before the *stegosaurs* and *ankylosaurs* roamed the earth!

And plenty of non-*Thyreophorian* dinosaurs had armor too. Complex and interesting defense systems can be found all over the Age of Dinosaurs; with such fierce predators roaming the lands, no dinosaur could afford to be totally unprotected. This section covers some of the lesser-known *Thyreophora* members, along with some of the strangest examples of body armor ever seen!

A group of Scelidosaurus,
Nothronychus and Argentinosaurus
dinosaurs graze on trees and leaves.

45

DUNKLEOSTEUS TERRELLI

DUN-kel-OS-tee-us

REGION: Canada, USA, western Europe, Morocco

SIZE: Up to 35 feet long

AGE: 360 - 380 million years

DIET: Carnivore

SCIENCE BITE: This enormous predator used the bony jaw plates in its skull to cut up prey—rather than rows of sharp teeth—making up for the fact that it was probably not a fast swimmer. This massive fish gets points for using its armor to hunt rather than defend itself. *Dunkleosteus terrelli* was heavily armored all around—being ripped apart by a bigger *Dunkleosteus* was its only threat!

ELGINIA MIRABILIS

EL-gin-ee-ah

REGION: Scotland

SIZE: 2 feet

AGE: 252 - 254 million years

DIET: Herbivore

SCIENCE BITE: *Elginia mirabilis* is a small member of the *Pareiasaur* family, reaching only two feet compared to the usual ten. Most of what scientists know of this ancient creature has come from just a single skull, which boasts sharp horns protruding from the base of its neck. These tiny lizards may have not used the horns for protection, but as *pareiasaurs*, they still would have had tough *osteoderms* protecting them.

49

SCUTELLOSAURUS LAWLERI

SKOO-tell-oh-SAWR-us

REGION: USA (Arizona)

SIZE: 5 feet long

AGE: 196 million years

DIET: Herbivore

SCIENCE BITE: An ancient member of *Thyreophora*, this little dinosaur spent most of its time on its hind legs and likely used its forelimbs for feeding. Its long tail likely helped it balance while eating this way. Named "little-shielded lizard," *Scutellosaurus lawleri* had long rows of *osteoderms* running down its back—more evidence that balance would have been impossible without such a long tail.

SCELIDOSAURUS HARRISONII

SKEL-eye-doe-SAWR-us

REGION: United Kingdom

SIZE: 13 feet long and 550 pounds

AGE: 183 to 196 million years

DIET: Herbivore

SCIENCE BITE: Another ancient *Thyreophorian*, *Scelidosaurus harrisonii* was significantly larger than its cousins in Arizona. This *quadruped* had *osteoderms* running down the length of its body, though scientists have debated their degree of spikiness. Since its discovery in the 1850s, *Scelidosaurus* has been categorized as both a *stegosaur* and an *ankylosaur*; while it more closely resembles an *ankylosaur*, it is no longer a member of either family.

TRUE OR FALSE

1. **T/F** The average human is taller than a *Stegosaurus*.

2. **T/F** All *Ankylosauria* have clubbed tails.

3. **T/F** If attacked, the *Stegosaurus* could fight back with its spikey tail.

4. **T/F** All armored dinosaurs were herbivores.

54

5. **T/F** The Jurassic Period came before the Cretaceous Period.

6. **T/F** All armored dinosaurs lived on land.

7. **T/F** *Thyreophora* were so short because they had to quickly scurry away from predators.

8. **T/F** Amazingly, fossils have even been found on Antarctica!

9. **T/F** The tails of *Ankylosaurs* could break the bones of even a T. *rex*.

10. **T/F** *Nodosauria*'s ultimate defense was a turtle-like spikey shell.

GLOSSARY

Ankylosauria
This group includes ankylosaurids and nodosaurids.

Ankylosaurid
Members of the Ankylosauria family. These dinosaurs had a large tail club and armor nearly from head to toe.

Biped
Animals who walk on two legs.

Carnivore
A meat-eating animal.

Fossil
The remains or trace of an animal from the past that has been preserved.

Herbivore
A plant-eating animal.

Nodosaurid
Members of the Ankylosauria family. Although they were similar to ankylosaurids, they did not have a tail club, but instead had bony bumps and spikes on their armor.

Osteoderms
Bony deposits underneath the skin that formed hard scales, spikes, plates, and even helmets.

Pareiasaur
Herbivorous reptiles with osteoderms covering their bodies.

Predator
An animal that hunts and eats other animals.

Prey
An animal that is hunted as another's food.

Quadruped
Four-legged animals.

Sauropods
Four-legged, herbivorous, lizard-hipped dinosaurs with long necks and tails.

Scute
A bony or horny plate or large scale.

Stegosauria
A group of armored dinosaurs famous for their spikey tails and rows of plates on their backs.

Thagomizer
The spikes on the tails of stegosaurs.

Thyreophora
A subgroup of dinosaurs with armor along their bodies. The armor includes scutes, osteoderms, spikes and plates. Suborders of this group include Anklosauria and Stegosauria.

IMAGE CREDITS

ABOUT THE AUTHOR

Patrick Scafidi is an author and editor living in Brooklyn, New York. He owes his love of dinosaurs to his parents, who made sure he never ran out of dinosaur books growing up, and to Jeff Goldblum, for teaching him that life finds a way. His favorite dinosaur is the *Allosaurus*.

ABOUT
APPLESAUCE PRESS

Good ideas ripen with time. From seed to harvest, Applesauce Press crafts books with beautiful designs, creative formats, and kid-friendly information on a variety of fascinating topics. Like our parent company, Cider Mill Press Book Publishers, our press bears fruit twice a year, publishing a new crop of titles each spring and fall.

Write to us at:
PO Box 454
Kennebunkport, ME 04046

Or visit us on the web at:
www.cidermillpress.com